DAUGHTERS
OF FIRE

DAUGHTERS OF FIRE

HEROINES OF THE BIBLE

By Fran Manushkin

Illustrated by Uri Shulevitz

SILVER WHISTLE

HARCOURT, INC.

San Diego   New York   London

www.harcourt.com

Silver Whistle is a trademark of Harcourt, Inc., registered in the
United States of America and/or other jurisdictions.

Library of Congress Cataloging-in-Publication Data
Manushkin, Fran.
Daughters of fire: heroines of the Bible/Fran Manushkin; illustrated by Uri Shulevitz.
p.   cm.
"Silver Whistle."
Includes bibliographical references.
Summary: Ten stories about women of the Hebrew Bible who influenced
the course of Jewish history through their courageous actions.
1. Women in the Bible—Juvenile literature.   2. Bible stories, English—O.T.
[1. Women in the Bible.   2. Bible stories—O.T.]   I. Shulevitz, Uri, ill.   II. Title.
BS575.M326   2001
221.9'22'082—dc21   98-29090
ISBN 0-15-201869-7

C E G I K J H F D B

Manufactured in China

The illustrations in this book were done in mixed media on paper.
The display type was set in Charlemagne.
The text type was set in Aldus.
Color separations by Bright Arts Ltd., China
Manufactured by South China Printing Company, Ltd., China
This book was printed on totally chlorine-free Enso Stora Matte paper.
Production supervision by Sandra Grebenar and Ginger Boyer
Designed by Ivan Holmes

For the heroic women of my havurah:
Lynn Blacker, Susan Green, Beth Handler, Ruth Joseph,
Anne Millman, and Maxine Wolf
—F. M.

To Esther and Walter Hautzig
—U. S.

Contents

INTRODUCTION

The Hebrew Bible is filled with stories of heroic girls and women. When I was a girl, I knew about only one of them: Queen Esther. My three brothers were all sent to religious school, but girls were not, which is why it wasn't until early adulthood that I learned about the many Biblical women whose actions changed the course of history.

Sarah, Rebecca, Miriam, and Deborah were God's prophets: Each was given a vision of the future, which she then helped bring to fruition. The women of the Exodus stand as an inspiration of collective action: Together they defied the cruel decrees of the Egyptian pharaoh, ensuring the survival of their people.

The Hebrew Bible does not offer us faultless heroes and heroines. It is not afraid to show us believable and flawed girls and boys, and men and women. If God had waited for perfect prophets, the wait would have been very long!

The story of Ruth and Naomi, who shared a profound faith and loyalty, is one of the most beloved in the world. But the Hebrew Bible also tells us about the rivalry of Leah and Rachel, and of Hannah and Peninah. Two of the matriarchs of the Jewish people, Sarah and Rebecca, were compelled to make painful decisions: Was Sarah justified in her treatment of

Hagar and Ishmael? Could Rebecca have acted with less deception in fulfilling God's role for Jacob? These stories have been cherished—and their questions argued over—for thousands of years.

The narratives of these tales first appeared in the Torah—the five books of Moses—the Scrolls, the Writings, the Prophets, and the Psalms. These stories were expanded and reinterpreted by sages and rabbis in the oral tradition, and then written down as folklore and in collections such as the Talmud and Midrash. I have learned much about Biblical men and women from these sources, but the stories collected here also contain interpretations of my own.

The brave and fierce women of the Hebrew Bible give us much to ponder about loyalty, love, and faith. Each of them embodies sparks of the divine spirit: They are *all* Daughters of Fire.

EVE

How sweet is the light,
how pleasant for eyes to behold the sun.
—*Ecclesiastes 24:5*

BEFORE GOD'S VOICE THERE was nothing, nothing at all. "Let there be light!" God commanded, and with these words God kindled the world. Sunlight shone forth upon the surface of the deep and sparkling seas, and upon the earth, spinning, spinning.

"Let this earth sprout seed-bearing plants and fruit trees of every kind," God declared, and it was so. The sun illumined the day, and the stars, the night, and a silver moon rose up, ready to do God's bidding.

Soon the sea sparkled with glittering fish and the sky with singing birds. "Let the earth abound with every kind of living creature and wild beast," God commanded. And it was so. God's love brought everything to life, and God called all of it good.

On the sixth day of creation, God called forth a miraculous well, a source of living water that would wander the world at God's will.

Gazing upon the earth, God then said to the angels, "I desire a help-mate for my world. Let us make a human after our likeness." Gathering forth dust of red and brown and white and yellow, from all corners of the earth, God shaped one human with *two* faces, female on one side, and male on the other.

Gently God blew into the human's nostrils the breath of life, saying, "You shall be named Adam, for you came from *adamah,* the dust of the earth."

On the seventh day, God ceased all work, calling *this* day holy and a blessing for all time. God named this day the Sabbath.

God placed the first human in a beautiful garden, in Eden, saying, "Adam, till this garden and tend it. You may eat from every tree except for the Tree of Knowledge of Good and Bad. You may *not* eat from *that* tree, for if you do, you will die."

Gazing around the garden, Adam stood alone—the only human on earth. "It is not good for you to be alone," God said gently. "Let us find you a mate." God caused every living creature to come before Adam:

Lambs and wolves marched by in peaceful procession.

Leopards and gazelles leaped gracefully.

Baboons and gorillas swaggered and chattered.

Every beast that crawled and ran and roared upon the earth showed its face to Adam, who named them, every one.

"Elephant!" said Adam.

"Zebra!"

"Gnat!"

Each of these creatures was wonderful to behold, but none was a fitting mate for Adam.

Gazing upon Adam's male and female faces, God said, "I shall make you a perfect mate." After casting a deep sleep upon the first human, God removed one of Adam's sides, and from this fashioned a woman, giving her Adam's female face.

"Awaken now," God said, and Eve opened her eyes. With her first gaze, she saw the Garden of Eden and Adam, asleep. God awakened him, and when Adam beheld Eve, he cried joyfully, "At last! *This* one is bone of my bone and flesh of my flesh."

Eve smiled upon Adam in perfect trust and love.

"My world rests upon deeds of kindness," God proclaimed. "Come, angels, we shall give Adam and Eve a wedding." God plaited Eve's lovely hair with pearls, and adorned her as a bride. Then God led her to the Tree of Life, and there, beneath its fragrant canopy, God pronounced the wedding blessings. Eve responded in a voice as sweet as music, the first human song on God's earth.

All of the angels joined in Eve's song, playing upon their harps and drums, and dancing in a glittering circle around the bride and groom. Ah, never again would the world see such a wedding!

Truly, Adam and Eve delighted in each other, and God delighted in them, clothing the couple in a Cloud of Glory. And for their wedding gift, God created a celestial golden light, by which they could see the entire world in one glance.

How eagerly Eve embraced God's creation! She explored Eden ardently, savoring the sweet scent of flowering almond trees and golden jasmine, and the sight of pomegranates as red as flame. She tasted of blackberries and mangoes and sunflower seeds, eagerly sharing each with Adam.

Indeed, Eve thirsted for knowledge of everything. When she discovered God's well of living waters, she gazed into the deeps and for the first time beheld her own face. How happy she looked! How hopeful!

In perfect trust Eve spoke with every living creature, each in its own language: Honeybees and eagles delighted in Eve's company, as did every shy snail and owl. There was no creature that Eve feared—*none* of them, large or small.

Alas, even in Eden there were serpents! And of all the animals, the serpent was the shrewdest. He walked upright, boldly pacing the garden. With his sly narrow eyes he watched Adam and Eve, growing ever more envious of their joy.

The serpent sidled over to Eve, saying, "Come! Taste of the Tree of Knowledge of Good and Bad."

Eve refused. "God told Adam we may not eat of or touch this tree, for if we do, we will die."

Upon hearing this the serpent smiled wickedly, for God had *not* forbidden Adam to *touch* the tree, only to eat from it.

The serpent smiled at Eve, urging, "Come! Touch the tree. You will *not* die."

When Eve refused again, the serpent pushed her against it.

"See?" he hissed. "You touched the tree and did not die. If you eat of this fruit, God knows, you will have every kind of knowledge."

Eve so yearned for knowledge and every source of wisdom that she ate of the fruit. She gave some to Adam, who also ate. The moment Adam tasted of the fruit, the Cloud of Glory departed from the couple, and they saw that they were naked. Covering themselves with fig leaves, Eve and Adam hid away among the trees.

"Where are you?" God called to Adam.

Adam answered, "I was afraid, so I hid."

"Did you eat of the fruit I had forbidden you to eat?" God asked, hoping Adam would admit to the deed.

Adam did not. Instead, he turned to Eve and said, "*She* gave me the fruit."

God thundered, "I gave Eve to you as a helpmate, and you are ungrateful to accuse her. You should *not* have eaten the fruit!"

God then asked Eve, "What have *you* done?"

She replied, "The serpent fooled me, and I ate."

"For this," God raged at the serpent, "you shall no longer stand upright but shall crawl on your stomach, and all of the food you eat shall be dust!"

To Eve, God said, "You shall bear your children in pain, and yet you shall desire your husband."

And to Adam, God declared, "The earth shall sprout thorns and thistles for you. And you shall earn your bread by the sweat of your brow."

Because Adam and Eve had not lived in harmony with God, they were banished from Paradise. But God did not destroy the Garden of Eden: It exists to this day, guarded by fierce cherubim who hold ever-burning swords of flame.

All her life Eve remembered the glories of Eden, for to have lived in Paradise, if only for *one* day, is a blessing forever. Eden's celestial golden light endures as well: To find a glimmer of this light today, you need only gaze at the Sabbath candles kindled by Eve's daughters.

Paradise awaits our return, when once again we live in harmony with one another and with God. Indeed, the Holy One created a plan to bring this about. It would begin, like Eden did, with *one* man and *one* woman— Abraham and Sarah.

SARAH

He who finds a wife has found happiness
and has won the favor of God.
—*Proverbs*

IN THE LAND OF UR OF THE Chaldees lived a woman so lovely she was called Sarai, which means "princess." She was said to resemble Eve, so radiant was her face and spirit. Certainly Sarai possessed a glad heart. But beware! She also had a temper—as fiery as flame.

Sarai could not abide harm to any of God's creatures. If her father dared raise a stick to his flocks, Sarai would shout, "Stop!" and fiercely stay his hand.

Sarai had many suitors, for any man who wed her would surely be blessed. They offered her flourishing vineyards, fields of the richest wheat, and olive groves, and gold and silver beyond counting.

But to each man, Sarai replied firmly, "No!" For she loved her kinsman Abram. Was he wealthy? Not a bit. And neither was he handsome. Abram was big and burly, and fierce as a bear, but his heart was as tender as Sarai's.

Many a morning before the sunrise, Sarai would venture out to the hillside to greet the newborn day. She would often come upon Abram there, keeping watch over his father's flocks. As the rising sun gilded the

fields with flame, the gentle voices of Abram and Sarai blended with the songs of awakening doves.

On one such morning, when God opened the heavens like a curtain, Abram asked of Sarai, "Do you ever wonder who created the heavens and the earth?"

Sarai replied, "Yes, I do."

Emboldened, Abram declared, "The sun shines so brightly, I once believed that *it* was God."

"Many people worship the sun," responded Sarai, "and the moon, too. But the sun disappears each night and the moon dims each day, so they cannot be God."

Abram smiled, saying, "Sarai, you are right! None of these is God: Only the one who made *all* of us is God."

"Yes," Sarai agreed, "and only a loving God would give us such a beautiful world."

But when Abram and Sarai descended from the hills, they saw people worshiping the sun and the moon, offering sacrifices to them. Abram's own father was selling clay idols in the marketplace.

Coming upon one of his father's customers, Abram asked him, "Sir, how old are you?"

"Seventy," the man replied.

"You are seventy?" Abram shouted. "And yet you purchase an idol made this morning?" Enraged, Abram raised his fist—and shattered the idol to bits. Seeing the old man trembling in fear, Abram said gently, "Do not be afraid, for God was not in that idol. If you wish to see God, you need only gaze into another's eyes."

How deeply Sarai felt the truth of Abram's words. So close in spirit were she and Abram, they felt as if they shared one soul. Soon they married—a marriage that was made in heaven, for God had planned it before they were born.

Abram made Sarai a tent with four openings, to the north and to the south and to the east and west: This enabled them to see and welcome all weary travelers. Abram would gently wash the dust from their feet, while Sarai restored them with tasty stews and fragrant bread.

Whenever Abram felt heavy of heart, Sarai's good humor cheered him. Indeed, he often told her, "My dear wife, in the darkest night I can always find you: I have only to follow your laughter."

Abram and Sarai shared every secret of their hearts. One night Abram confided, "Sarai, I have heard the voice of God. We have been commanded to leave this land and go to a place God will show us. God has promised that we shall be made into a great nation."

Without hesitation, Sarai responded to Abram, "We will abide by God's command."

And so Abram and Sarai became wayfarers, placing their trust in God. They would come to be known as the Hebrews—a word that means "from the other side"—for they would cross many rivers and many lands.

Wherever Sarai and Abram journeyed, they beheld people worshiping idols. Abram would thunder, "Men, be wise! These clay figures are not God."

Sarai would say to the women, "This is not the worship God wants."

Everywhere the couple went, they turned the hearts of people to God. Soon thousands of families joined them on their journey.

When Abram and Sarai reached the land of Canaan, God commanded, "Raise up your eyes and look around you, for I give all the land you see to you and your offspring." This was the Promised Land, and it was as lovely as Eden. Sarai marveled at its gardens of cucumbers and apricots, and its fields of ripening wheat. Fallow deer and oryx roamed the hills, and oleander and wild thyme scented the air. Indeed, Canaan seemed to be a land of milk and honey.

But no sooner had Sarai and Abram put up their tents than a famine struck. All of the crops blackened and died, and then every animal breathed its last.

"We must leave Canaan until the famine is over," Abram told Sarai. They began journeying on foot toward Egypt, where food was plentiful. As Sarai trod the rocky paths, swirling dust stung her eyes and the blazing sun beat down without mercy. When Sarai saw a stream of cool, clear water, she joyfully waded in to splash the dust away.

Beholding his wife's lovely face reflected in the water, Abram warned her, "Sarai, the Egyptians are not God-fearing people. When they see how beautiful you are, they will kill me and take you away. Tell them you are my *sister*, not my wife. Indeed, it would be better if they do not see you at all."

And so Sarai hid away in a chest that was meant to hold wheat. Four men hoisted it upon their shoulders and carried it to the Egyptian border.

"What have you in that chest?" the sentry demanded.

"Barley," said Abram.

"Barley is not so heavy," the sentry replied, growing suspicious. "Are you sure it is not wheat?"

"Very well," Abram blurted. "I will pay the tax on wheat."

"You are much too eager," the sentry sneered. "Are you sure you are not carrying gold?"

"I will pay the tax on gold then!" Abram said wildly.

Hearing this, the sentry demanded, "Open this chest at once!"

With trembling hands, Abram slowly raised the lid, and as the sunlight touched Sarai's face, all of Egypt was illumined. "Ah, you are a treasure," the sentry sneered. "Guards, take her to Pharaoh's harem."

To her horror, Sarai was flung upon the back of a camel, which hurried her to Pharaoh's palace. Boldly Sarai spoke up to God: "You have commanded us to leave our land and we have obeyed. Be merciful, God, and do not let Pharaoh touch me."

God heard Sarai and responded, "Do not be afraid."

When Sarai reached the palace, seven servants bathed her in rose water and dressed her in a gown of the finest red silk. They then escorted her to Pharaoh, a man worshiped as God on earth. "Ah, you are lovely!" Pharaoh said, and he rose from his throne and eagerly approached her.

Holding God's promise close to her heart, Sarai remained serene. "Ah," murmured Pharaoh, "you are so regal. I must embrace you at once!" As he drew closer, the radiance of his golden crown almost blinded Sarai. But when Pharaoh reached out to touch her, his hand was stopped— by an angel.

Falling to his knees, Pharaoh cried, "God must be with you." Thereupon he set Sarai free, and bestowed upon her jewels and herds of cattle and camels. "Go with Sarai!" Pharaoh commanded his daughter, Hagar. "She is so blessed, it is better to be her servant than a princess."

And so Sarai and Abram were reunited. They soon returned to the Promised Land, for the famine there had ended. So blessed was Sarai that God's presence hovered over her tent night and day in a Cloud of Glory. Each time she kindled her Sabbath lamp, the flame burned all the week long, and the bread made by Sarai's hands remained always warm and fragrant.

"Look to heaven and count the stars," God declared to Abram, "and so numerous shall your offspring be." Indeed, God renamed the couple Abraham and Sarah, saying, "I shall bless Sarah and give you a son by her, and I will maintain my covenant with him."

But ten years passed, and the couple was not blessed with a child. Sarah, resolving to fulfill God's promise, told Abraham, "Go to my handmaiden Hagar, and she shall bear a child; we shall be built up through her."

Abraham refused, so much did he love Sarah. But finally she prevailed, and Hagar gave birth to a child, a son they named Ishmael.

Thus, the years passed, and although Sarah and Abraham grew very old, they still cared for wayfarers, offering all comforts to them.

One night three strangers appeared at their tent. One of these—in truth the angel Michael—made a mark on the wall, saying, "In one year, when the sun crosses this line, Sarah will be with child."

Sarah laughed. She was ninety years old!

God's voice thundered, "Sarah, why do you laugh? There is nothing I cannot do!"

"I did not laugh," said Sarah, trembling.

"Yes, you did!" God said.

That very night Sarah's youth was restored to her! Every wrinkle was smoothed away, and her body became strong and supple.

"Look!" Abraham shouted. "My gray hair has turned black." He, too, was young again—leaping around like a newborn lion.

As time passed, Sarah's stomach grew as round as the moon, and then she gave birth to a son. He was named Isaac, which comes from the

word *laughter*. "God has brought me laughter," Sarah declared. "Everyone who sees will rejoice with me."

Sadly, Isaac's brother, Ishmael, did not rejoice. As Isaac grew into boyhood, Ishmael aimed arrows at him with his bow, saying each time, "I was only pretending."

Seeing this, Sarah began fearing for Isaac's life. Her anger flared up and she demanded, "Abraham, send this boy and his mother away."

Abraham, who loved both of his sons, refused. But God commanded him, "Abide by all that Sarah says. It is through her and Isaac that you shall become a great nation. But I shall also care for Ishmael and his mother. Ishmael, too, shall lead a great people."

So Abraham sent Hagar and Ishmael to the wilderness, and as God had promised, an angel watched over them. The angel sustained them with water from the wandering well, which God had called forth on the sixth day of Creation.

Many years later, God gave Abraham another command, saying, "Abraham, take your son and offer him as a burnt offering on the heights that I shall show you."

As always, Abraham sought to obey God, but the moment he raised his knife to his son, an angel stayed his hand; for it was Abraham's obedience God had wanted, not any harm to Isaac.

When Sarah discovered that her son had indeed been saved, she gave a great cry, and then she died.

Sarah lived a long life—127 years. She is remembered to this day as the mother of all the Children of Israel. The day that Sarah died, all of the miracles departed from her tent. They were soon to be restored—when her son, Isaac, married Rebecca.

REBECCA

The day is short; the task is great.
—*Pirkei Avot, Ethics of the Fathers*

REBECCA LIVED IN ARAM-Naharaim, and she had the great misfortune to be born into a family of scoundrels. Her father was the laziest man in the village, and as for her brother, Laban: He was a sly and treacherous thief.

While Rebecca toiled in the sun, tending to lost lambs and stray calves, her father slept in the shade of an olive tree. And what was her brother, Laban, doing? Stealing the neighbors' sheep!

Everyone in the town loved Rebecca, who was a gentle and generous girl. Watching her among her rascally family, many a villager would whisper, "Rebecca, you are a rose among thorns."

By the time she grew into womanhood, Rebecca had observed every human folly. With one quick glance, she could read each person's soul.

Happily, there was one place in Aram-Naharaim where Rebecca found solace: among her friends at the village well. In the heat of the summer, its cool, fresh waters offered the women a taste of heaven. Indeed, this well had been in Eden—for it was God's eternal wandering well, now given another task to perform.

At dusk every evening, when Rebecca drew water for the evening meal, she also drew forth news of her friends. One by one, each was wed to a man from an honorable family. Rebecca was left to wonder sadly, "Who would choose to be kin to *me*?"

One day she received her reply. An old man came to the well leading a caravan of camels. He commanded the camels, "Kneel!" Rebecca watched in sympathy as the great shaggy beasts knelt in exhaustion, their mouths open, gasping for water.

Although Rebecca was adept at reading character, she could not read minds. So she did not know that this old man was Abraham's servant, Eliezer, coming to seek a wife for Isaac.

Closing his eyes, Eliezer prayed, "God, grant me good fortune in my task. I will ask these girls to lower their jars so I may drink. The one who replies, 'Drink, and I will *also* water your camels'—may *she* be the one you have decreed to marry Isaac. Then I will know that you have dealt kindly with him."

When Eliezer opened his eyes, he saw Rebecca, and he asked her, "Please, may I sip a little water?"

"Yes," said Rebecca, hastening to lower her heavy jar from her shoulder. As Eliezer drank his fill, Rebecca added in her kind voice, "I will also draw water for your camels."

To Rebecca's astonishment, the old man gazed at the heavens with a great wide smile. The well also burst forth with enthusiasm. The moment Rebecca lowered her jar to be filled, the waters bubbled up to meet her! Rebecca filled her jar again and again, pouring the water into the drinking troughs. A camel's thirst is not easily quenched—and there were ten of them!

When this task was completed, Eliezer asked, "Is there room in your father's house to shelter for the night?"

"Yes, of course," Rebecca said, "and we have straw and feed for your camels."

At this, Eliezer proclaimed, "Praise God, who has guided me to this house and to you." Then, to Rebecca's amazement, Eliezer placed golden bracelets upon her wrists and adorned her with glittering rings. When Rebecca's brother, Laban, saw these, he smiled upon the old man, welcoming him warmly.

Eliezer told Laban the purpose of his visit: "I wish to bring Rebecca to my master, Abraham, so that she may marry his son Isaac."

Rebecca's gentle heart began pounding furiously, and she watched Laban closely for his reply.

"How many flocks of sheep and cows has your master?" Laban asked.

"Too many to count!" said Eliezer. "And Isaac shall inherit them all."

"Well then," declared Laban, "take the girl and go!"

Rebecca's face flushed with joy. "Can this be true?" she asked herself over and over. "Shall I be wed to an honorable man?"

Rebecca paid little heed to the many bridal gifts that Eliezer lavished on her and her family. "I am going! I am going!" she exulted, and her friends rejoiced with her.

But the next day, seeking yet more gifts, Laban sought to delay Rebecca's departure, telling Eliezer, "It is *our* custom to ask a woman's permission before she is wed. Rebecca, will you go?"

"I will!" she replied without hesitation. Pleased by her great eagerness, God performed another miracle for Rebecca: Her camel journey to

Canaan, which *should* have taken seventeen days, was accomplished in only three hours!

Upon entering Canaan, Rebecca beheld a man walking in a field. So gentle was his face that he looked like an angel. "He is to be my husband!" Rebecca knew it at once. And so startled was she that she tumbled off her camel!

As Isaac rushed over to assist her, Rebecca modestly placed a veil over her face. Although he could not see her, the mere touch of Rebecca's hand restored all joy to Isaac's life: For three years he had been mourning his mother's death. But now his sadness lifted.

Indeed, the moment Rebecca stepped into Sarah's tent, all of its miracles returned: Again a Cloud of Glory hovered over the entrance, and when Rebecca kindled the Sabbath candles, the flames burned all the week long. Isaac savored the bread Rebecca made, for each wheat and barley loaf remained always fragrant and warm.

Rebecca grew to love her husband. Clearly Isaac was a kindly man who saw goodness in every man's face. The couple prayed together for a child to carry on the covenant with God, a son who would lead the next generation.

But when Rebecca finally conceived, her joy swiftly turned to despair, for she felt bitter turmoil within her womb. She entreated God, "Tell me, what is wrong?"

"There are *two* nations in your womb," God responded. "One people shall be mightier than the other, and the older shall serve the younger."

Rebecca pondered these words as she awaited the birth of the twins. The firstborn was covered with a mantle of thick red hair and ruddy skin, and he was named Esau.

His younger brother emerged holding fast to Esau's heel, and he was named Jacob, which comes from the word meaning "heel."

Esau, as the oldest, would by custom receive a birthright from his father, giving him the greater portion of the family's wealth.

As the years passed, Rebecca observed her two sons closely. Esau grew into a mighty hunter. No deer was safe from his bow. Isaac, who savored the tasty venison Esau prepared from his hunts, came to favor him.

Jacob was a quiet and inward boy, and Rebecca favored him. Of course, Jacob desired his father's love as well. One day he decided to please Isaac by cooking his favorite dish: spicy red lentil stew.

As the stew's delicious scent filled the air, Esau ran into the tent, ravenous with hunger. "Give me some food to gulp down!" he demanded.

Jacob replied, "First, give me your birthright."

"You may have it," said impulsive Esau. "Just give me this food." Thus Esau sold his birthright—for a bowl of soup!

God continued to bless the family with bountiful flocks. Rebecca noted well each of her sons' characters, holding in her heart God's prophecy for them. Rebecca also loved and cared for Isaac as he grew ever more old and frail.

As the years passed, Isaac's eyes began to weaken, and soon he could barely see. Believing that his death was near, Isaac made ready to give his blessing to his oldest son.

Calling Esau to his side, Isaac instructed him, "Take your quiver and bow and hunt some game for me. After you have prepared the meat, I will give you my innermost blessing."

Hearing this, Rebecca began to tremble, for it was Jacob who was meant to receive the blessing. Rebecca summoned Jacob, saying, "Go quickly and choose two goats from among our flocks. I will prepare a meal. You shall take it to your father, and he will bless *you*."

Terrified, Jacob protested, "Esau is hairy and I am smooth-skinned. My father will know I am trying to trick him! And he will give me a *curse*, not a blessing."

Rebecca stood firm. "Let the curse be upon *me*. Do as I say."

Rebecca found Esau's clothing and placed it upon Jacob. Then she covered his smooth hands and neck with the two goatskins, saying, "When Isaac embraces you, the scent of the hunt will be on your clothes, and you will feel hairy, like Esau."

Rebecca gave the bowl of stew to Jacob, but his hands trembled so much he could barely hold it. God sent two angels, and they held Jacob steady.

When Jacob stepped into Isaac's tent, his father asked, "Which one of my sons are you?"

"I am Esau," said Jacob. "Sit up, Father, and eat of my game so you may give me your blessing."

"Come closer," Isaac replied, "so I may feel you, my son."

Jacob drew near, and his father gently felt his arms and neck, saying, "The voice is the voice of Jacob, but the hands are the hands of Esau." Even so, Isaac ate the stew and drank the wine. He then placed his hands upon Jacob's head and declared, "May God give you the dew of heaven and an abundance of wine and grain, and may your mother's sons bow to you."

As Jacob departed, Esau entered with his offering of food.

"Who are you?" asked Isaac.

"I am Esau, your firstborn," he said.

Isaac began to tremble, asking angrily, "Who is it then who brought me game, and whom I blessed? *He* is the one who must *remain* blessed!"

Hearing this, Esau burst into bitter sobbing. "Have you but one blessing to give?" he cried. "Oh, Father, bless me, too!"

Isaac responded: "You shall enjoy the fat of the earth, yet by your sword shall you live, and you shall serve your brother."

Esau was so embittered that he vowed to slay his brother. Rebecca perceived this and made another heartbreaking decision: She told her beloved Jacob, "You must flee from our home."

Isaac agreed with Rebecca's plan, telling Jacob, "Go to Haran and choose a wife there from among the daughters of Laban, your mother's brother." Isaac once again blessed Jacob, saying, "May God make you fertile and numerous, and grant you the blessing of Abraham, so you may possess the land that God gave him."

As Rebecca embraced Jacob one last time, she said hopefully, "In time, Esau's fury may subside, and perhaps he will forgive you." Indeed, Rebecca's wish *would* come to pass and the brothers one day would be reconciled.

It was through Rebecca's actions that God's destiny for Jacob was assured. It was he—with all his faults—who could best lead the next generation. And so Jacob went to Rebecca's village to seek a wife.

LEAH AND RACHEL

Sustain me with raisins, revive me with apples,
for I am faint with love.
—*The Song of Songs*

Leah and Rachel were Rebecca's nieces, the daughters of her thieving brother, Laban. To be Laban's sister was surely a misfortune, but to be his daughters was a disaster!

Leah, the older of the two, was a bold and adventurous child, with the gentle eyes of a dove. She was eight years old when her sister, Rachel, was born. Rachel's first cries were loud and long. Indeed, she seemed never to stop. Neither warm milk nor her mother's caresses could soothe her.

Leah's tender heart went out to the child, and she sought every way to cheer her. She brought her yellow irises and daffodils to gaze upon, and soft sheepskin to caress her skin. But still Rachel wept inconsolably.

Leah searched the darkest caves, where the bees hid their sweetest honey. Defying their stings, she scooped up the dripping honeycomb and brought it home to Rachel. "Taste of this," Leah whispered, placing the nectar on Rachel's lips. The child tasted the honey, and her crying ceased; and for the very first time, she smiled.

"See?" said Leah softly. "Life is sweet."

As the years went by, Leah became more of a mother to Rachel than their own, who was always occupied with her thieving husband. The two sisters became inseparable, and each night they shared a bed, and their deepest dreams as well.

As Leah grew into womanhood, she would often ask Rachel, in the darkness of night, "Which man do you think I shall marry?"

Rachel would reply, "An excellent man! One who is worthy of you."

Soon after one of these conversations, Laban announced proudly, "Leah, I have found you a wealthy husband. You shall marry your cousin Esau."

"Esau?" Leah gasped. "He is a hunter, a rough man."

Rachel also protested: "Esau cares *only* for killing! He is not the right man to marry my sister."

Enraged, Laban stamped his foot, shouting, "Leah *shall* marry Esau!"

At this, Leah's tears began to flow, and day and night they did not cease. Leah wept as she kneaded the bread, and she wept as she added mint to her father's tea. And all the time, she prayed to God, "May it be your will that I marry a *different* man, and not Esau."

God responded to Leah's prayer and placed another woman in Esau's path, and so he married her.

But the bitter tears Leah had shed weakened her beautiful eyes. They grew pale and clouded, and soon the sunny world Leah cherished so dearly became a realm of shadows.

As Leah's beauty faded, Rachel's grew ever greater. Sunlight burnished her skin to a golden bronze, and Leah plaited Rachel's dark hair into a lovely braid, which flew behind her as she ran through the fields.

Rachel would often find herself drawn to the village well, where her aunt Rebecca had encountered Isaac's servant Eliezer. Often, at moonrise,

Rachel would gaze deeply into this well. Seeing her face reflected next to the moon, she would wonder, "Shall *my* fate be decided here, too?"

At twilight one day, Rachel received her reply. She saw a young man approaching the well. He was dressed so shabbily he looked like a tramp.

This man asked the shepherds gathered there, "Do you know Laban, the brother of Rebecca?"

"Yes," the men said, "and there is his daughter Rachel, tending his flocks."

When this stranger—in truth, Rachel's cousin Jacob—set eyes upon Rachel's radiant face, he stepped forward, declaring, "I shall draw water for your animals."

"Wait!" the shepherds warned. "The wellstone is heavy, and requires the strength of seven men to lift it."

But Jacob seized hold of the stone—and up it came as if commanded! And then the waters bubbled up to meet Jacob's hands.

Rachel, startled and delighted, smiled upon Jacob. It was such a smile, Jacob was utterly love-struck and he kissed her! Then, astonished at his boldness, Jacob fell to weeping.

Rachel rushed away, her face as red as sunrise, to find her father. Laban greeted Jacob eagerly, remembering well the riches of Jacob's father, Isaac.

"Welcome!" Laban gushed, and he kissed Jacob's cheeks, hoping to feel gems hidden there. No, no gems.

Then Laban hugged Jacob, patting his pockets in search of jewels. No, no jewels! "Ah well," Laban sighed with less enthusiasm. "Come and take shelter under our roof."

That night during the evening meal, Rachel and Jacob said little, but ah, their eyes spoke much! Neither took any notice of Leah.

The next day, Jacob agreed to work for Laban, tending his few and sickly flocks. "Just because you are my kin," said Laban, "shall you serve me for nothing? Tell me, what shall I pay you?"

Jacob declared, "I will serve you seven years—for your daughter Rachel."

"Ah, well." Laban shrugged. "It is better she wed *you* than anyone else."

And so, out of love for Rachel, Jacob taught himself to become a man of the fields. Scorching heat ravaged him as he tended Laban's flocks by day. On many a moonless night Jacob rescued lambs and calves from the jaws of hungry wolves.

Rachel delighted greatly in Jacob, but her joy was tempered by sorrow for her sister, Leah. Time and again Laban brought suitors for Leah; but each, upon seeing Leah's weakened eyes, would shake his head and depart.

Finally, when Jacob's seven years were fulfilled, he said to Laban triumphantly, "Give me my bride so that I may marry her."

Laban arranged a boisterous wedding—with much drinking of spiced wine. At nightfall Jacob gently drew his veiled bride into his tent, all perfumed with cinnamon and myrrh. There in the delicious darkness, Jacob called his wife "Rachel," and she answered, "Yes."

But at dawn, when the sun's first rays touched his wife's face, Jacob saw that it was Leah! In a rage, he ran to Laban and demanded, "Why did you deceive me?"

Laban replied casually, "In *our* place, it is customary for the oldest daughter to wed first. But if you agree to serve me *another* seven years, you may also marry Rachel."

"I will," Jacob declared, so much did he love her.

Thus the two sisters were fated to share one husband. Is it any wonder they soon became rivals?

Leah grieved bitterly, for she knew Jacob loved Rachel. God, responding to Leah's sadness, blessed her with four sons, so that her husband might come to honor her.

Rachel remained childless and, growing envious of Leah, told Jacob, "Give me children or I will die!"

Jacob cried, "I cannot take the place of God, who alone can give you children."

In desperation Rachel gave her handmaiden, Bilhah, to be with Jacob, and she soon bore him two sons. For a little while, Rachel felt triumphant.

But the sisters' rivalry was only beginning. Responding to Rachel, Leah gave *her* handmaiden, Zilpah, to Jacob, and *she* bore him two sons. God also granted Leah two more sons, and a daughter she named Dinah.

Finally God blessed Rachel with a child, a boy she named Joseph.

All this time God increased not only Jacob's children but the flocks he watched as well. After serving Laban for fourteen years, Jacob told him, "Let me return now to my homeland."

"No! Stay!" Laban insisted. "Because of you my flocks have flourished." He then added grandly, "I shall give you flocks of your own: every newborn animal that is speckled and spotted."

Laban knew well that these births were rare. Ah, but God responded by bringing these animals in great numbers. Jacob's flocks quickly increased: by a thousand rams and a thousand ewes and a thousand goats each month! He soon was a wealthy man.

God commanded Jacob then, "Return to the land of your kindred, and I will be with you."

Jacob told this to Leah and Rachel, asking, "Will you go with me?"

"Yes!" said Rachel. "Our father has sold us, and we are nothing to him."

Leah agreed, saying, "The wealth God has given belongs to us and to our children. Let us go to your land."

Rachel and Leah had come to love Jacob's God, and they no longer worshiped idols. Before departing, Rachel stole into Laban's tent and removed his idols, thinking, "How can I leave him to worship these?"

And so, on a day when Laban was away shearing his sheep, the sisters fled from their father's house. They and Dinah and their handmaidens, Bilhah and Zilpah, rode upon the backs of camels, with their eleven sons walking behind them.

Through the years, Rachel and Leah had spoken but rarely, so great was their enmity. Now, riding side by side, the sisters persisted in silence.

But when they reached the Promised Land, Rachel could not help marveling at its beauty: "Ah, the sun is as golden as honey!" Without realizing she had spoken aloud, Rachel added, "And the cedar trees! They soar so high!"

Leah, responding eagerly, said, "Tell me more!"

"I see doves, with silver wings," Rachel answered. "And olive trees and date palms . . . and poppies, so *many* red poppies!"

"This land is lovely!" Leah said with tenderness, for Rachel's words had brought each hill and valley to life. Soon the two sisters spoke not only of doves and poppies, but of themselves and their deepest hopes for their children. Shyly Leah reached out for Rachel's hand, whispering, "Sister, how I have missed you."

"And I, you," Rachel replied, taking her sister's hand. She then confided, "Leah, I am with child."

"I will be your midwife and care for you," Leah promised.

When Laban discovered that his daughters had fled, he pursued them to Gilead, to the hill country, and demanded of Jacob, "Why did you steal my daughters? And where are the household gods you took?"

Jacob, not knowing that Rachel had taken her father's idols, replied angrily, "On my honor, I did not take a needle or knife. May the person who took your idols not remain alive!"

Laban searched all of Jacob's tents, but Rachel had hidden the idols beneath her camel cushion. Rachel sat upon this cushion, and so the idols were never found. Defeated, Laban made peace with Jacob and departed.

When Rachel began feeling the first pangs of childbirth, she gave a loud cry and Leah rushed to her side. Hour after hour Leah held and comforted Rachel, and finally, at dawn, she gave birth to a healthy boy.

"Here is your son," said Leah, placing the child in Rachel's arms. Rachel embraced him and smiled at Leah. Then her soul departed and she died.

Leah and Jacob were plunged into grief. When Jacob discovered that it was Rachel who had stolen her father's idols, he sobbed, "It was through *my* words that she died!"

Can comfort be found after so many tears? As Leah cradled Rachel's son, God sought to ease Jacob's grief by revealing a vision of the future: This road, where Rachel was to be buried, would be the path their descendants would travel during their exile. Upon seeing them, Rachel would weep for her children, and God would always respond by bringing them home.

Through their many children, Rachel and Leah and Bilhah and Zilpah became the mothers of the twelve tribes of Israel. Their descendants would increase, as God had promised, and their names are honored forever and remembered as a blessing.

THE WOMEN OF THE EXODUS

Tears may linger for a night,
but joy comes with the dawn.
—*Psalm 30*

THE DESCENDANTS OF RACHEL and Leah and Bilhah and Zilpah would come to be known as the Children of Israel. Here is how this happened:

Late one night, as Jacob and his wives journeyed to the Promised Land, Jacob was set upon by a stranger, who began wrestling with him. They struggled the entire night, and at dawn it was Jacob who prevailed.

Clasping the stranger, Jacob demanded, "I will not let you go until you bless me!"

"You shall no longer be called Jacob, but Israel," proclaimed the stranger. Jacob gasped! Now he realized he had been wrestling with an angel, for the word *Israel* means "wrestling with God." This is why Jacob's descendants are called the Children of Israel.

For many years the Israelites thrived in the Promised Land. But when a famine struck, they, like their ancestors, sought refuge in Egypt, where the harvests were plentiful.

The Egyptian Pharaoh dealt kindly with them, because of Rachel's son Joseph. God had given Joseph a wonderful gift: He was able to read dreams. By interpreting Pharaoh's dreams, Joseph foretold the future, saving the Egyptians from many a peril. "The spirit of God resides in this man," Pharaoh proclaimed, placing Joseph in command of the entire land.

But when many years had passed, and Joseph and Pharaoh died, a new Pharaoh emerged. This one did not know Joseph, and when he saw how numerous the Israelites had become, he grew frightened. "If there should be a war," he said, "these people may join my enemies and fight against me. I shall reduce the number of Israelites by forcing them into slavery." Now, instead of herding flocks, the Israelites would toil in Pharaoh's brickworks, making bricks for his cities.

Pharaoh issued another command: "All Israelite men must sleep in the fields, away from their wives. Thus no children will be born to them and this people will cease to exist."

Ah, but Pharaoh was no match for the Israelite women! They refused to let their people die. Each day they did Pharaoh's bidding, toiling in his brickworks, but at sundown they defied him! They bathed themselves in the river, washing away the dust of the day. Then gazing into copper mirrors, they adorned their hair with fragrant night flowers.

They waited for the moon to hide behind the clouds, and then under cover of night, the women hastened to the fields. As the moon emerged, they awakened their sleeping husbands, and the men, beholding their lovely wives, joyfully embraced them.

Gazing up at the sky together, the Israelites remembered God's promise: "I will make you a people as numerous as the stars."

Thus the brave Israelite women continued having children. Enraged, Pharaoh commanded the Hebrew midwives, Shiphrah and Puah, "Kill each newborn boy."

But the midwives *also* defied Pharaoh, and every child lived. Desperate, the Pharaoh commanded his people, "Every Israelite boy baby must be drowned in the Nile!"

Upon hearing this, an Israelite named Amram made a difficult decision. He divorced his wife, Jochebed, saying, "Now we will have no sons for Pharaoh to kill!"

But their six-year-old daughter, Miriam, protested, "Father, your decree is worse than Pharaoh's. *He* wants to kill boys, but *you* are not allowing girls to be born either."

"That is true," Amram said sadly.

"You must remarry Mother," Miriam insisted. "She is destined to have a child who will set our people free!" So powerful were Miriam's words that Amram knew they had come from God. Amram did remarry Jochebed, and Miriam danced joyfully at the wedding, singing and playing her timbrel.

Within a year Miriam's prophecy was fulfilled: A son was born, and at the sound of his first cry, the house filled entirely with light.

Amram joyfully kissed Miriam, saying, "Daughter, all you say is coming true." Jochebed knew, though, that if the Egyptians found her son, he would be drowned. She built a small ark for him and, placing him inside, floated the ark upon the Nile. "I am obeying Pharaoh's orders by placing my son in the water—but he shall *not* drown."

Miriam hid away behind a tree, promising to keep watch over the child. Soon Pharaoh's daughter came to bathe in the river, and God chose that very moment to make the baby cry. Hearing his cries, the princess followed them to the ark. When she saw the Hebrew child, her heart melted, and she declared, "I will raise this child as my son." She then commanded her servants, "Find me a Hebrew nursemaid to provide him with milk."

"*I* can find you a nurse!" called Miriam, hurrying out of her hiding place. She soon returned with the perfect nurse: Jochebed, the boy's own mother.

The princess named the baby Moses, and she raised him amid great wealth in the royal palace. But as Moses grew into manhood, he learned of his heritage; and he never forgot his people.

One day Moses came upon a cruel taskmaster beating a Hebrew slave. Moses became so enraged that he killed the man. When Pharaoh heard of this, he demanded that Moses be slain. Moses left Egypt then, fleeing for his life.

As the years passed, the plight of the Israelites worsened, and they cried out to God. Hearing their pleas, God appeared before Moses in a burning bush, commanding, "Go to Pharaoh and tell him to let my people go."

Moses was terrified! "How can I lead the people to freedom?" he wondered.

But Moses obeyed God and returned to Egypt. When he told Pharaoh what God had commanded, the king thundered, "*I* am God here! And I will not let your people go."

God responded by inflicting plagues upon Egypt:

The Nile turned to blood.

Frogs and insects and wild beasts infested the land.

Pestilence and boils afflicted the people.

Still, Pharaoh refused to let the Israelites go.

A plague of hail descended, and locusts, and darkness as black as a raven's wing. *Still,* Pharaoh refused to let the Israelites go.

Then God sent the most terrible plague of all: Every firstborn of the Egyptians was slain. Pharaoh finally acknowledged the power of God, telling Moses, "Take your people away at once!"

So quickly did the Israelites depart that they had no time to prepare food or bake bread for the journey. The women carried their dough in kneading bowls upon their shoulders, and baked matzah: flat, unleavened bread. "Bring your drums and timbrels, too!" the prophet Miriam urged them. "God is performing miracles for us, and we shall soon thank God with joyful song!"

That night six hundred thousand Israelites began their journey out of slavery. God went before them—in a pillar of cloud to guide them by day, and a pillar of fire to light the night. When the Israelites reached the shore of the Red Sea, they heard the *hsssss* of the waves, and then another sound: horses' hooves!

"Pharaoh has changed his mind," cried the people. "He has sent his army to kill us."

"Raise your hand over the sea!" God commanded Moses. Moses obeyed, and God split the sea. A wall of water rose on either side, with a dry seabed between them. In awe the Israelites hastened across the Red Sea, arriving safely on the other shore.

"Pursue them!" Pharaoh told his army. "Drive your chariots into the sea."

God commanded Moses again: "Raise your staff." When he obeyed, God brought the walls of water crashing down, and Pharaoh's army perished.

With great emotion and gratitude, the Children of Israel offered up a song to God. "Who is like you?" they sang. "God will reign forever and ever." Miriam took her timbrels in her hand and led the women in song and dance.

Miriam's great prophecy had come true: Her people had been set free. In her honor, God's miraculous wandering well would accompany the Israelites wherever they went, sustaining them with its waters. It would now be called Miriam's Well.

Soon the Children of Israel would reach Sinai, where again they would behold God's great power. There they would also receive God's greatest gift, the Torah.

THE WOMEN IN THE WILDERNESS

How lovely are your tents, people of Jacob,
your sanctuaries, descendants of Israel.
—Numbers 24:5

THE CHILDREN OF ISRAEL were now free to worship God. But they found themselves in a barren land, indeed, a huge wilderness. Where were the fields of golden wheat? The blossoming vineyards? Around them they saw only sand, and rocks, and fearsome mountains reaching to the sky. How would they survive?

This is how: God fed them by raining down bread from heaven. It was called manna, and to each person it tasted like her favorite food. To some, it tasted of cucumbers; to others, of melons, ripe and juicy, or barley cakes with honey. Every morning the people would gather this manna; on the sixth day, God gave them a double portion so they would not have to work to collect it on the Sabbath.

The people journeyed deeper and deeper into the desert. On the third new moon, they arrived in the wilderness of Sinai, and they set up their camp there, at the base of the mountain.

It was then that God commanded Moses, "Come up to my holy mountain." After Moses ascended Mount Sinai, God declared, "Tell the Children of Israel: If you hearken to my voice and keep your covenant with me, you shall be to me a holy nation."

When Moses descended and told the people God's words, they responded, "All that God has spoken, we will do."

Three days later Mount Sinai began to shake. Thunder sounded and the mountain became wreathed with smoke. God had come down upon it, in fire.

Every man, woman, and child gazed up in silence and awe. The sea, too, fell silent, ceasing its mighty roar. The entire earth listened as out of the fire God proclaimed these Ten Commandments:

I am your god, who brought you out of Egypt. You shall have no other gods besides me.

You shall not make any idols and bow down to them.

You are not to use my name in vain.

Remember the Sabbath day and keep it holy.

Honor your mother and father.

You shall not murder.

You shall not commit adultery.

You shall not steal.

You shall not testify falsely against anyone.

You shall not covet your neighbor's house or wife or servant or ox or ass, or anything that is your neighbor's.

Once again God commanded Moses to ascend the mountain, and there he received these laws inscribed on stone tablets. A cloud covered the mountain, where Moses remained for forty days and nights. At the base of the mountain, the Israelites waited and waited.

"Where is Moses?" asked one of the elders. "Perhaps he has been burned by God's fire."

"Where is God?" cried another elder. "Has God abandoned us?"

As the desert winds howled, the people quaked in fright. "We must make an image of God!" they decided. "Let us melt down our gold and build a golden idol. Then we need not fear."

Many of the men offered up their gold, telling their wives, "Remove your necklaces and earrings so we may use them for the idol."

"No!" the women said, refusing. They held to God's commandment, declaring, "We will not worship idols!"

Miriam assured her people, "My brother Moses will return! He is like the moon, whose light is hidden in its dark stage. But like the moon, he will come back to us."

Still, the fearful men fashioned a golden calf. Then dancing around it, they sang, "*This* is our God, who has brought us out of Egypt."

Seeing this, God angrily told Moses, "Your people have turned away from me. They are bowing to a golden calf."

Moses descended from Mount Sinai, cradling in his arms the two stone tablets inscribed with God's words. When Moses beheld the Israelites worshiping the golden calf, he angrily flung down the tablets. As they shattered, the holy letters flew away, returning to God.

Moses destroyed the golden calf, and soon tribe turned upon tribe; many were slain. Then Moses entreated God, "Show mercy upon my people, in memory of their ancestors."

God did show mercy, and he summoned Moses, to give him the tablets anew, saying, "Build a sanctuary to hold my laws."

Grateful for God's mercy, the Israelites made an Ark hewn from acacia wood. The Ark was lined with gold, inside and out, and a golden Menorah was fashioned with seven branches, one for each day of the week.

This time the women were eager to offer up their gold. They gave their necklaces and rings and bracelets so that they might be melted down and made part of God's Ark. The women offered their copper mirrors, too, but Moses refused them, saying, "These were used as tools of vanity."

But God said to Moses, "These are *holy* vessels! The women used them to beautify themselves for their husbands, and to increase my children." And so the mirrors were accepted.

The women also wove tapestries for the Tabernacle, the tent that housed the Ark. So skillful were these women that they spun the wool while it was still on the goats! They also collected olive oil for the holy lamp and prepared fragrant spices for incense.

The Tabernacle resembled the hospitable tent of the people's matriarch, Sarah. Like her tent, it was blessed with God's Cloud of Glory, day and night, and the holy lamp, when kindled, remained burning for days.

Because the women had refused to worship the golden calf, they were also given their own holiday: the celebration of the new moon, Rosh Hodesh.

At Mount Sinai God had spoken to an entire people for the first time. With these Ten Commandments, the Children of Israel now had a way to bring justice to the world, and to help perfect God's creation.

DEBORAH AND YAEL

God shatters the cedars of Lebanon,
making the hills skip like rams,
the mountains leap like lambs.
—*Psalm 29*

THE CHILDREN OF ISRAEL dwelled in the wilderness for forty years, and it was a new generation who finally entered the Promised Land. Joshua, the great-great-grandson of Rachel and Jacob, led the Israelites into Jericho, where they fought and won a great battle. The Promised Land was not easily settled; many tribes and peoples claimed it.

In Bethel, at this time, there lived a woman named Deborah, which means "bee." Why was she called Deborah? Because she had a mighty sting!

Deborah possessed great wealth: She owned date palms in Jericho, rich vineyards in Ramah, and olive trees in Bethel. But her greatest wealth was her wisdom. How she excelled at settling disputes. Many a farmer and herder brought their conflicts before Deborah, and she would always resolve them. So much did the Israelites value Deborah's counsel that they chose her to be a judge.

Rare was it for any woman to be so chosen! In all seasons Deborah held court in the shade of a palm tree, and people who came to her in strife would depart in peace. Deborah also delighted in weaving wicks for the lamps of the Menorah at Shiloh, where the tablets of the Ten

Commandments were kept. With her deft hands, Deborah wove the wicks good and thick, so the holy light would shine on and on.

God saw Deborah's devotion and proclaimed, "Because you take pains to shed light in my house, I will let *your* light, *your* fame, shine abroad in the land!"

Sadly, at this time there was great strife in Canaan. Each night the ruffians of King Jabin raided the Israelites' orchards, pillaged their crops of wheat and barley, and seized their sheep and cattle. No Israelites dared to venture on the roads at night, lest they be robbed or murdered.

The leader of King Jabin's army was a fearsome general named Sisera. He was a gigantic man—so huge that when he bathed in the river, enough fish were caught in his beard to feed multitudes! Sisera's thunderous voice made leopards tremble in their tracks. Certainly no man dared to defy him.

Desperate, the Israelites cried out for God's help, and God responded. "I will send a woman to you, and she will shine as a light for you."

Deborah was chosen to be God's prophet. God revealed a great plan to her: a plan that would lead the Israelites to victory over their oppressors. Heeding God's call, Deborah summoned an Israelite soldier named Barak. She told him, "God commands you to gather ten thousand soldiers upon the top of Mount Tabor. When Sisera's army responds, God will deliver them into your hand."

The brave soldier trembled with fear. "Sisera's army has nine hundred chariots with nine hundred drivers and nine hundred archers. How can we defeat them?" Finally Barak agreed to Deborah's plan, telling her, "I will obey, but only if *you* come with me."

"Very well," Deborah replied. "But when victory comes, it will *not* be yours: God will give Sisera into the hands of a woman."

Deborah journeyed to every village, telling the Israelites, "You must unite into a single army and fight Sisera."

If Barak trembled at the mention of Sisera, the Israelite tribes cowered even more. "This task is greater than Joshua's conquest of Jericho," they argued. "Do not ask us to go."

But Deborah was so persuasive that many of the tribes agreed to her plan. Barak assembled ten thousand soldiers, and they ascended to the top of Mount Tabor. Below them on the plain came Sisera, leading a terrifying procession of nine hundred iron chariots carrying nine hundred drivers and nine hundred archers.

Barak shook like a palm leaf in a storm, but Deborah stood firm. At the moment God decreed, the Israelites began running down the mountain. As they ran, God sent fire pouring down from the heavens, and torrents of rain. The rain filled the River Kishon to overflowing, so that Sisera's chariots became mired in the mud.

The Israelites set upon the chariots and put every soldier to the sword. Sisera leaped from his chariot, fleeing for his life. Seeking a safe place to hide, he came upon a tent with a lone woman standing beside it.

Her name was Yael, and she welcomed Sisera, saying, "Come in and refresh yourself. I will bring you food and water, and you may rest here until evening."

Sisera hurried into Yael's tent, and, exhausted, he soon fell asleep. As dusk approached and the moon began to rise, Yael left the tent to milk her goats. As she did so, Yael prayed, "God, strengthen me against this enemy. Show me by a sign that you will come to my aid: Let Sisera awake and ask for a drink of water."

When Yael returned to her tent, Sisera *did* awake and ask for water.

Yael gave him a goatskin of warm milk instead, and after this lulling drink, Sisera resumed his sleep.

Gathering all the courage she possessed, Yael seized hold of her mallet with one hand and a wooden tent pin with the other. With one swing, she drove the tent pin into Sisera's head. He gave a great gasp and he died.

Trembling at her deed, Yael rushed from the tent. When she saw Barak running toward her, Yael cried out, "The man whom you seek is here."

When Barak entered Yael's tent, he proclaimed, "Deborah's prophecy has come true: The great Sisera has been slain by a woman."

After the battle, Deborah gathered all the Israelite tribes in a great assembly, and she offered up a song of gratitude to God. She praised the men who had joined in defying Sisera—and derided those who had not.

Because of Deborah, the Promised Land was at peace again. She contentedly resumed her calling as a judge, and her great light continued to shine upon her people. Indeed, these many peaceful years would come to be known as the Age of Deborah.

HANNAH

Out of the depths I call to You;
God, hear my prayer, heed my plea.
—*Psalm 130*

ANNAH'S NAME MEANS "grace," and she was truly endowed with this quality. She had a soft voice and a spirit as gentle as a summer breeze. Her husband, Elkana, doted on her, and the two were devoted to each other. They lived in the fertile country of Ephraim, where they nurtured their flocks and their groves of olives and almonds.

But as the years passed and Hannah did not bear any children, Elkana despaired, saying, "When we are old and frail, who will care for us? Who will be our posterity?" Hannah had no reply; she waited patiently for God to bless them with a child.

When none was born, Elkana felt he had no choice but to take a second wife, so *she* might bear him a child. He wed a woman named Peninah—and no crueler person ever lived! After she bore two healthy children, she began taunting the childless Hannah. In a sweet voice she would murmur, "Hannah, why are your fingers idle? You should be sewing a kerchief for your older son and a shirt for your little one."

How Hannah wept at these cruel taunts! But she held her tongue. Did Peninah stop? No! She persisted in her torments. Each day at dawn, she awakened Hannah, calling, "Wake up, lazy one! Wash your children's faces and prepare them for the day."

Still, Hannah never responded in anger. Elkana loved Hannah dearly and sought to comfort her with lavish gifts—with fine gowns and every kind of rare fruit and vine. These gifts enraged Peninah further, and consoled Hannah not at all: Only a child could ease her grief.

Every year, Elkana's family and hundreds of others made a pilgrimage to the Tabernacle at Shiloh, where the tablets of the Ten Commandments were kept. There the Israelites offered to God the first fruits of their harvest.

What a boisterous pilgrimage this was! Children ran in and out among the donkey carts, shouting and flushed with excitement. They wandered through the fields gathering irises and daffodils, filling their mothers' arms with flowers. At nightfall, all the families would light fires and share their evening meal. It was a time of great joy and fulfillment. But for Hannah there was no rejoicing.

When the happy crowds reached Shiloh, they hurried into God's sanctuary, where the Ark was kept. Only Hannah remained outside. There, her grief began pouring forth, and she prayed to God, "Of all the people you have created for your world, can you not give me *one* son?"

Emboldened by her own words, Hannah promised, "If you bless me with a son, I shall give him to you; and he will live here in your sanctuary."

As Hannah prayed, her lips moved, but her words were so soft, none but God could hear them. Seeing Hannah's lips moving but hearing no sound, a priest named Eli scolded her, "Woman, how long will you act like a drunk? Cease, and put away your wine!"

"I have not had any strong drink and I have sipped no wine," Hannah replied. "I have been praying out of the abundance of my grief."

The priest regretted his cruel words and, softening his voice, said, "Go in peace, and may God grant you what you have asked."

Indeed, God heard Hannah and blessed her with a child, and she named him Samuel, which means "God has heard me." And as Hannah had promised, she brought Samuel to Shiloh, to live there and to become one of God's priests.

Hannah was blessed with five more children, two daughters and three sons. Each year she would collect the finest wool from her flocks and weave a warm robe for Samuel. When her family visited Shiloh, Hannah would joyfully embrace her son and place the new robe upon his shoulders. This son would become one of the wisest men in the land, chosen to anoint the Israelites' first kings, Saul and David.

Hannah lived a long life of love and fulfillment with her husband and children. Her solitary prayer at Shiloh was the first prayer to be offered at the house of God—instead of a sacrifice of first fruits and flocks. It is *this* prayer from the heart that God most cherishes, and that remains an inspiration to this day.

RUTH AND NAOMI

I would feed you with the richest wheat,
with honey from the rock would I satisfy you.
—Psalm 81

IN THE SPRINGTIME, THE
Promised Land bursts into flower. Sweet-scented roses fill the hillsides,
and the song of the turtledove delights the ear. Spring is the time for the
first harvest; the ripening barley waits in the fields.

In the region of Judah, one village surpassed all others in fertility, and
so it was called Bet Lechem, which means "house of bread." In Bet Lechem
there lived a woman called Naomi, whose name means "sweet one." She
was a hardworking and pious woman, married to Elimelech, a prosperous
farmer. They had two sons, Mahlon and Chilion.

Sadly, wealth can grow wings and fly away. One year the rain refused
to fall, and the ground yielded no grain. Still, Elimelech's family had
plenty of food, for he possessed storehouses bursting with wheat.

One night Elimelech told Naomi, "I fear that the poor may descend
on us and take our food. Our family must leave Bet Lechem at once."

Riding on surefooted donkeys, Naomi and her husband and sons
crossed the Jordan River and the River Arnon, and entered the Land of
Moab.

For a time the family flourished, but suddenly, without warning,
Elimelech sickened and died. Soon after this, Naomi's sons married two

Moabite princesses, named Orpah and Ruth. They shared a roof with Naomi, who treated them warmly, and for many years all went well. Ten years passed and neither Orpah nor Ruth was blessed with children. Then the family's wealth began melting away, as quickly as springtime snow: Their flocks of sheep and goats sickened and died, and then, most tragically, Naomi's sons, Mahlon and Chilion.

Who can measure such a terrible grief? Naomi and Ruth and Orpah wept together, finding comfort in one another. When the mourning period was over, the women grew yet more fearful. Without husbands, they would have no one to protect them from the world's perils. What would their futures hold?

Naomi, who had always been docile and accepting of her fate, was suddenly filled with resolve. She told Ruth and Orpah, "I shall go back to Bet Lechem!"

The two young women protested, "The journey is dangerous, and you have no animal to ride."

"I must go," Naomi insisted. The next morning she arose early, before dawn, as did her daughters-in-law so they might walk with her part of the way.

When they reached the River Arnon, and the sun was gilding the sky, Naomi kissed Ruth and Orpah, saying, "Go back now to your mother's house, and may God deal kindly with you, as you have with me. God grant you rest in the house of your new husbands."

Orpah and Ruth fell to weeping, and they said, "We will return with you to your people."

"Go! Turn back!" Naomi insisted. "Have I husbands who will care for you? Go back to your country and to your god."

Orpah agreed, and she kissed Naomi and turned back toward Moab.

But Ruth stayed, saying, "Do not entreat me to leave you, for wherever you go, I shall go! Wherever you lodge, I shall lodge; your people shall be *my* people, and your God, *my* God. And may I be punished if any but God part me from you."

Naomi argued no further. She took Ruth's hand in hers, and together they descended from the hills of Moab into the fiery oven of the desert. Soon their bare feet grew blistered and bloody, and scorpions and vultures awaited their every misstep.

Finally Ruth and Naomi beheld the green hills of Bet Lechem. It was springtime and, everywhere, the sunbirds were singing and golden barley was ripening in the fields.

"Ah, your land is lovely," Ruth said, smiling.

When the townswomen saw the once wealthy Naomi clad in rags, they asked, surprised, "Can *this* be our sweet Naomi?"

Naomi said, "I am bitter now; do not call me sweet."

But Ruth assured her, "I will go and seek food for us, gleaning in the fields."

It was God's command that the farmers in the Holy Land should not harvest the crops in the corners of their fields. These they were to leave for the poor. Also, if the farmers dropped grain as they picked it, this, too, had to be left for the poor.

When Ruth went out to glean, God led her to the field of Boaz, a kinsman of Naomi's. Although Boaz was a wealthy man, and no longer young, he toiled in the fields beside his men. When he saw Ruth there, Boaz asked his workers, "Who is this woman?"

"Her name is Ruth," they told him. "She has come from Moab with her mother-in-law, Naomi."

Gently Boaz called to Ruth, "Come and partake of our midday meal."

Ruth was startled, and as she joined Boaz, she asked, "Why have you taken such notice of me—a stranger?"

Boaz smiled as he filled her plate with food and replied, "I know of your kindness to Naomi, and how you left your own land to come to a people you do not know. May God reward you greatly."

Ruth said no more. At the completion of the meal, Boaz whispered to his men, "When you cut the barley, pull out some stalks and leave them on the ground for Ruth."

That evening Ruth returned to Naomi with an apron overflowing with grain. When Ruth said that she had gleaned it in the fields of Boaz, Naomi's face lit up with joy. "Blessed be Boaz!" she said. "He is our kinsman, my daughter. And blessed be God who has sent us to him. It is well that you remain in Boaz's field."

And so, each day, Ruth returned there to glean. Her dignity and modesty so impressed Boaz that he told himself, "Any young man who weds her will be blessed."

One day near the end of the harvest, Naomi drew Ruth close and said, "Daughter, I seek rest for you, and shelter and happiness. Heed, now, what I say. Tonight after you return from the fields, bathe and anoint yourself and put on fresh clothing. Follow Boaz to the threshing floor and hide away until he is asleep. Then quietly place yourself at his feet. When Boaz awakens, he will know what to do."

Ruth replied without hesitation, "All that you tell me, I will do."

And so under cover of velvet night, Ruth ventured out to the fields.

She watched as Boaz ate and drank his fill of wine and then, contented, fell into a restful sleep.

Silently Ruth drew near to Boaz. At midnight, when the moon emerged from the clouds, Boaz awoke and saw—a woman. "Who are you?" he asked.

"I am Ruth," she said softly. "Spread your robe over me, for you are my closest kinsman."

Boaz rose joyfully. "May God bless you, for this act of kindness is greater than any other! You could have chosen a younger kinsman to marry you. Indeed, there is a man who is closer kin to you and Naomi. If he refuses to fulfill this duty, I will gladly marry you."

Ruth returned to Naomi with Boaz's promise. Naomi embraced her warmly, saying, "Boaz will not rest until he settles this."

As he had promised, Boaz hurried to find Naomi's younger kinsman, and in front of all of the people at the city gate, he asked him, "Will you marry Ruth?"

"No," said the man, refusing. "For it is customary that if we should have children, they will carry Ruth's first husband's name and not my own."

"Then *I* shall marry her!" Boaz said gladly.

Boaz and Ruth were married at once. The townswomen prayed, "May God make Ruth like Rachel and Leah, who built up the house of Israel."

Soon God blessed Ruth with a son, whom she lovingly placed in Naomi's lap. As Naomi cradled her grandson, the townswomen named the child Obed, saying, "Blessed be God who has revived your life, Naomi, for this boy is born of your daughter-in-law Ruth, who loves you and is better to you than seven sons." Naomi helped Ruth care for Obed, who was a joy to her all her life.

In time, Obed grew up and married and had a son, Jesse. He, too, had a son, David, who became the king of Israel. And that is how Ruth the Moabite became the great-grandmother of kings.

QUEEN ESTHER

You will step on cobras,
tread safely on lions and serpents.
—Psalm 91

HE ISRAELITES FLOURISHED
in the Holy Land for hundreds and hundreds of years. They created a
splendid Temple in Jerusalem, where they housed the tablets of the Ten
Commandments. The great golden city of Jerusalem became a place of pilgrimage and the center for the worship of God. All day, all night, the light
of the great Menorah blazed for all to see.

These glorious years would end tragically. The Temple was beset by
enemies from within and without, and it was destroyed. The Israelites
were sent into exile—and the survival of their faith was in jeopardy.

One of the exiled tribes was that of Judah, and because of this the Israelites came to be known as the Jews. Many Jews were sent to live in Persia, under the rule of King Ahasuerus. He was a cruel and impulsive man
who commanded 127 provinces and all the armies of Persia and Media.

How the king loved to flaunt his power and wealth, holding court in
his magnificent palace in the city of Shushan.

One day the king resolved to give a glorious banquet, the grandest
since the creation of the world. He ordered his royal seamstresses to sew
silken tapestries to adorn the marble columns of his garden. The royal car-
penters built massive tables to hold the huge platters of venison, lamb, and

pigeon pies. Hundreds of silver bowls were filled to overflowing with luscious grapes and the sweetest melons.

"Now my guests may arrive!" the king commanded. Of course, the guests were duly impressed. They reclined on luxurious couches, sipping wine from golden goblets, and very soon they grew intoxicated, as much by the scent of the roses as by the wine.

Did this banquet last one day, or two? No! It lasted for a week! On the seventh day, King Ahasuerus, fierce with wine and self-importance, boasted, "My queen, Vashti, is the most beautiful woman in the world! I shall bring her before you to dance." But when the king's chamberlains commanded Vashti to appear, she refused, remaining in her chambers.

"Where is my queen?" thundered the king. So furious was he at Vashti's rebellion that the king commanded his men, "Banish Vashti!" And the deed was done.

"Now *no one* in my kingdom will dare to defy me," the king boasted, "and all the women of Persia will obey their husbands."

Soon, though, the king grew lonely, and he sought another woman to be queen. He told his couriers, "Go to each of my one hundred and twenty-seven provinces, and from each bring me the loveliest woman. From among these I shall choose a *new* queen, beautiful and obedient."

The 127 couriers commenced their search, unaware that the loveliest woman in Persia lived near the castle in Shushan. She was named Hadassah, which means "myrtle." Hadassah had curly black hair and eyes as radiant as stars. She was an orphan who lived with her cousin Mordechai. Hadassah was a timid and sheltered girl who knew little of the ways of the world. Rarely did she venture from her own garden.

When she heard of the king's command, Hadassah was terrified and hid herself in the darkest corner of her house. Many other women of Persia did the same, for who would want to be queen to *this* king?

When his 127 couriers informed Ahasuerus that many women were concealing themselves, he raged, "Anyone who hides from me will be killed!"

Now Hadassah had no choice but to present herself before the king. Her cousin Mordechai warned her, "Do not reveal that you are a Jew, for there are people here who would harm us." Indeed, to disguise her identity, Mordechai gave Hadassah a new name, Esther, which means "hidden."

Soon the 127 most beautiful women in Persia were assembled inside the palace. Vain and proud, they were attired in glorious silken gowns of every color of the rainbow, and in pearls and diamonds.

One alone wore a plain, modest dress, befitting her guileless spirit. Ah, but Esther's beauty could not be denied. "*You* are the loveliest in the land!" proclaimed the king. He placed the golden crown upon Esther's head, and taking her trembling hand, sat her next to him upon the throne.

Never was there a more reluctant queen! All Esther wished to do was return home. She missed her cousin Mordechai and her people as well. She daily sent Mordechai secret messages, and on the Sabbath, alone in her chambers, she kindled the lamps.

Mordechai often tried to catch a glimpse of Esther by lingering in the palace's outer courtyard. It was there that he overheard two chamberlains plotting to kill the king. Quickly, Mordechai sent word of this to Esther, who told it to her husband. "Hang these villains!" the king roared; and the deed was done and duly recorded in the royal chronicles.

Now the king appointed a new chamberlain, named Haman. He was a cruel man, bloated with pride. He took great pleasure in riding through the city on horseback, demanding that all his subjects bow to him.

One man refused—Mordechai. He insisted, "Haman is a man like any other. I bow only to God."

Haman became enraged and told the king, "There is a certain people who do not keep the king's laws. If it pleases you, let it be written that all these people be murdered."

The impetuous king agreed and wrote out this proclamation: "On the thirteenth day of the twelfth month, all the Jewish people in my one hundred and twenty-seven provinces shall be slain—women, men, children. Everyone!"

The king's horsemen brought this decree to all 127 provinces. When the Jews heard it, they fell into despair, weeping and tearing their clothes in mourning. They fasted, and day and night offered prayers to God.

Mordechai did not give up hope. He wrote this message to Esther: "You must go to the king and beg him for our lives!"

When Esther read his note, she burst into tears. "I am terrified of the king's wrath," she replied to Mordechai. "I must not approach my husband unless he summons me. Anyone who appears to him unbidden can be put to death!"

Mordechai responded, "Have you not become queen so that you may save your people?"

Esther's heart was moved by these words. She paced her royal chamber in anguish, fasting and praying and seeking strength from God. "If I do not reveal to the king that I am a Jew, then I will live," Esther said, "but my people will die."

Gathering up all her courage, Esther decided. "I will go to the king, and if I perish, I perish!" As she hurried from her chamber, a plan began unfolding in her mind.

When Queen Esther approached the first of the king's seven courtyards, the guard called out, "Surely, you are not going to the king without being summoned?"

"I am," Esther replied.

She entered the second courtyard. "When the king kills Esther, I will take her jewels," murmured the guard.

She reached the third courtyard. "When the king kills Esther, I will steal her royal robes," declared the guard there.

Esther's heart pounded as she proceeded through the fourth and the fifth and the sixth of the king's courtyards. Finally reaching the one nearest the king, Esther prayed, "God, do not be far from me."

Upon seeing Esther's radiant face, King Ahasuerus could not help but smile upon her. He took her hand and asked, "My queen, what do you wish? Anything you request, I will give you, even half of my kingdom."

"If it please you," Esther replied, "call Haman so that I may tell *both* of you what I want."

When Haman appeared, Esther said graciously, "I request that my king and Haman attend a banquet I shall prepare. At that time, I will reveal my wish."

"Your request is granted!" said the king.

That night Haman bragged to his wife, "Queen Esther prefers only me and the king to dine with her. But all of this means nothing to me—for Mordechai, who refuses to bow to me, is still alive!"

Haman's wife, who was as hateful as he, offered this reply: "Let a gallows be built, and ask the king to hang Mordechai from them. Then your feast will be joyful."

"I shall do it," Haman shouted.

On the evening before the banquet, the king was restless and could not sleep. On such occasions he would ask a servant to read aloud from his royal chronicles. How the king relished hearing stories of his victories!

The servant began to read: "A plot to kill the king was discovered by a loyal subject named Mordechai. He revealed this plot to Queen Esther and saved the king's life."

"Ah, yes," remembered the king. "Tell me, what great honor was Mordechai given for this deed?"

"None," replied the servant.

"None?" shouted the king. "I shall provide one for him."

At that moment, the king heard a noise in his garden. "Who is that?" he asked.

"It is Haman," replied the servant, for Haman was building the gallows to hang Mordechai.

The king summoned Haman and asked him, "How shall I reward a loyal subject?"

Thinking the king wanted to reward *him*, Haman replied, "Let him be dressed in royal robes and paraded on horseback so that all shall honor him!"

"A fine idea," the king agreed, and he made Haman lead Mordechai in honor throughout the town!

On the next day, Haman arrived at the palace, eager to enjoy Queen

Esther's banquet and forget the humiliation of the previous day. After he and the king partook of her delicious feast, the king asked Esther, "Now, tell me, my queen, what is your wish?"

Esther replied, "If I have found favor with you, let my life be spared as well as all of my people's, for we are to be slain!"

"Who would dare kill you and your people?" shouted the king.

"*This* wicked man, Haman!" said Esther boldly, pointing her scepter at him.

"My queen, have mercy!" Haman cried, flinging himself at Esther's feet. Trembling, he clutched desperately at her gown.

"How *dare* you touch my queen!" the king thundered. He ordered his guard, "Take Haman away and kill him!"

The guard answered, "Haman built a gallows for Mordechai, who saved the king's life."

"Hang Haman from it," roared the king. As Haman was taken away, Mordechai arrived. The king smiled upon him, saying, "*You* are now the master of Haman's house!" The king also placed Mordechai above all his courtiers.

Esther rejoiced at her reunion with Mordechai, but her task was not yet complete. She told the king, "If you do not reverse your decree, all of the Jews will be slain."

"My decrees cannot be canceled," insisted the king. "But I shall issue a *new* decree: All the Jews in Persia may rise up and slay anyone who tries to harm them!"

This new edict was swiftly brought to all 127 of the king's provinces. The Jews began preparing for the fateful day, and when it arrived they fought valiantly and they defeated their attackers.

To mark this great occasion for all time, Queen Esther and Mordechai established a festival named Purim, from the word *pur*, which means "lots," for Haman had cast lots to decide the day of the Jews' deaths.

Purim is a noisy holiday, on which the story of Queen Esther is told aloud. Each time Haman's name is mentioned, all the people drown it out with noisemakers and raucous shouting.

So may it be with *all* oppressors: that they be loudly defied!

Afterword

The women in these stories have given the Jewish people many of their most cherished traditions and holidays. They are listed below.

Lighting the Sabbath Candles

The Jewish Sabbath begins just before sundown on Friday night, when the woman of the house kindles the Sabbath candles. After she does so, she says this blessing: "Praised are you, Adonai, our God, ruler of the universe, whose mitzvoth add holiness to our lives and who gave us the mitzvah to kindle Sabbath light."

Family Blessing for Daughters

After lighting the Sabbath candles, parents place their hands on the heads of their daughters and say, "May God give you the blessings of Sarah, Rebecca, Rachel, and Leah."

The Veiling of a Bride

Brides wear veils today because Rebecca modestly placed a veil over her face upon first seeing Isaac. Also, because Jacob was tricked by a veil into marrying Leah instead of Rachel, there is a wedding ritual called the bedecken: Before the groom walks down the aisle, *he* places the veil on his bride's face. He may then proceed to the wedding canopy, confident that he will be marrying the right woman.

The Passover Seder

In honor of the prophet Miriam, there is a new tradition of placing a goblet of water, called Miriam's Cup, on the seder table. Miriam is associated with water because she watched over Moses when he was placed in the Nile, because she led the women in song and dance after the miraculous crossing of the Red Sea, and because she inspired God to rename the miraculous wandering well of water Miriam's Well.

The Blessing of the New Moon (Rosh Hodesh)

Rosh Hodesh honors the women in the wilderness, who refused to worship the golden calf. On these days, women pray and study, sharing special meals and rituals. Sometimes they light a floating candle, which looks like the moon floating in the sky. Women also bake round bread—loaves in the shape of full, round moons. Mothers and daughters share the joy of this day together.

Rosh Hashanah

Sarah's story is told in synagogues on Rosh Hashanah, as is Hannah's. Hannah's fervent, silent prayer is a continuing inspiration for all prayers on the High Holy Days.

Shavuoth

The story of Ruth and Naomi is told every year on Shavuoth, a festival that takes place at the time of the harvest. Shavuoth celebrates the day that God gave the Torah to Israel—a Torah that Ruth, the convert, loved and cherished.

Purim

Esther's story is told every year on Purim. Children come to this noisy, joyous occasion in costume. Girls often dress up as Queen Esther and some wear Queen Vashti costumes, to honor the queens who defied the king.

ACKNOWLEDGMENTS

I am grateful for the assistance I have received from many people as I wrote and researched this book. I heartily thank my skillful and valiant editors, Linda Zuckerman, Rachel Goldberg, Paula Wiseman, and Tamson Weston; my wonderful agents, Amy Berkower and Jodi Reimer; and the following people who helped me with my research and fact-checking: Eileen Shmidman, Marin Waxman, Liza Stabler, Deborah Hautzig, Esther Hautzig, Rabbi Melinda Panken, Rabbi Yael B. Ridberg, and Rabbi Hara Person. I also would like to express gratitude to my writers group members: Harry Mazer, Norma Fox Mazer, Doris Orgel, Bonnie Bryant, Miriam Cohen, Sandra Jordan, Peter Lerangis, Ellen Levine, Barbara Seuling, and Marvin Terban, for their blessed good humor.

BIBLIOGRAPHY

These Biblical stories were derived from many sources, ancient and modern. I began with the Torah, of course, which I read in several different translations. Other sources are listed below.

Berrin, Susan, ed. *Celebrating the New Moon: A Rosh Chodesh Anthology*. Northvale, N.J. and London: Jason Aronson Inc., 1996.

Büchmann, Christina, and Celina Spiegel, eds. *Out of the Garden: Women Writers on the Bible*. New York: Ballantine Books, 1994. (I am especially grateful for Cynthia Ozick's essay on Hannah.)

Frankel, Ellen. *The Five Books of Miriam: A Woman's Commentary on the Torah*. New York: G.P. Putnam's, 1996.

Frankiel, Tamar. *The Voice of Sarah: Feminine Spirituality and Traditional Judaism*. New York: Biblio Press, 1990.

Ginzberg, Louis. *The Legends of the Jews*. Philadelphia: Jewish Publication Society of America, 1909, 1910, 1911, 1913, 1956. (This book was my greatest source for folklore and legend.)

Harlow, Jules, ed. and trans. *Siddur Sim Shalom: A Prayerbook for Shabbat, Festivals, and Weekdays*. New York: Rabbinical Assembly: United Synagogue of America, 1989.

Jewish Publication Society of America. *The Writings: Kethubim*. Philadelphia: Jewish Publication Society of America, 1982.

Kates, Judith A., and Gail Twersky Reimer, eds. *Reading Ruth: Contemporary Women Reclaim a Sacred Story*. New York: Ballantine Books, 1994.

Magriso, Yitzchok. *Exodus*. Vol. VII of *The Torah Anthology*. Translated by Aryeh Kaplan. New York and Jerusalem: Moznaim Publ'g Co., 1981.

Plaut, W. Gunther. *The Torah: A Modern Commentary*. New York: Union of American Hebrew Congregations, 1981.

Sarna, Nahum M. *Exodus: The Traditional Hebrew Text with the New JPS Translation. The JPS Torah Commentary*. Philadelphia: Jewish Publication Society, 1991.

———*Genesis: The Traditional Hebrew Text with the New JPS Translation. The JPS Torah Commentary*. Philadelphia: Jewish Publication Society, 1989.

Steinsaltz, Adin. *Biblical Images: Men and Women of the Book*. New York: Farrar, Straus & Giroux, 1984.